THE 3-D CLOCK

Stephen Claughton

The 3-D Clock

© Stephen Claughton

First Edition 2020

9074359801SBN: 978-1-907435-98-0

Stephen Claughton has asserted his authorship and given his permission to Dempsey & Windle for these poems to be published here.

Author's photograph ©Cynthia Nolan

All rights reserved. No part of this publication may be reproduced, stored in a retrieval system or transmitted in any form or by any means without the written consent of the author, nor otherwise circulated in any form of binding or cover other than that in which it is published and without a similar condition being imposed on a subsequent purchaser.

Published by Dempsey & Windle
15 Rosetrees
Guildford
Surrey
GU1 2HS
UK
01483 571164
dempseyandwindle.co.uk

British Library Cataloguing-in-Publication Data

A catalogue record for this book is available from the British Library

Printed in the United Kingdom by CMP Ltd, Poole, Dorset

*In memory of my mother
Beryl Mai Claughton
(1921-2016)*

Acknowledgements

Acknowledgements are due to the editors of the following magazines, webzines and blogs in which some of these poems first appeared: *Against the Grain*, *Atrium*, *Ink Sweat & Tears*, *London Grip*, *Magma*, *The Poetry Shed* and *The Warwick Review*.

CONTENTS

Who's Who	7
Musical Ear	9
The Double	10
Home	12
Home Entertainment	14
Still Life	16
The 3-D Clock	18
Nonage	20
See Me After	22
Anomia	24
Con Moto	25
Mother Tongue	27
Voicemail	28
On the Ward	29
Opening the Window the Night You Died	30
Your Funeral	32

Who's Who

*"And can you tell me, please,
who is the current Prime Minister?"
You can't, of course. It's hard:
they change so often these days.*

*And anyway haven't you always
had trouble remembering names?
I think of that rigmarole
you used to keep going through,*

*when you'd rattle off a roll-call
of all the family's names,
including the dog's, a bitch,
before you registered mine.*

Musical Ear

Then there was the Welsh, male-voice choir
that followed you around. They'd been at it for weeks,
you said, arriving unannounced,
like a group of carol singers, at inconvenient times.

You hadn't minded at first. At least, their singing was good —
heavenly, you described it, better than all the choirs
you remembered from your childhood,
especially the solo tenor — out of this world.

The problem was you couldn't make them stop.
Instead you tried drowning them out,
la-la-la-ing away at the top of your voice,
just you versus all those men.

Or if that didn't work, you'd resort to the radio,
turning it up loud even at three in the morning —
fortissimo Radio 3, *fortississimo* Classic FM.
But either they were deaf, or they wouldn't take the hint.

I couldn't hear them, of course, but you still insisted I try.
We sat like a couple of kids sharing a set of headphones,
or as we'd been years ago with the wireless warming up
for "Listen with Mother" again.

You wouldn't accept that the voices were all in your head.
They'd sung "Land of my Fathers" in Welsh,
all three verses word perfectly throughout,
so how could it be you? You only knew the first two.

The Double

When I come to take you out,
you're expecting someone else.
"Who is it?" I ask, concerned
(the old are so vulnerable).
Oh, it's no one I know, you say,
just someone you've met somewhere
who drives you around in his car.
I check your diary to see,
but there's nothing there for today
except for the entry I made,
against which you've pencilled
five ticks and written "Important!"
above, doubly underlined.
You're glad it's me, you say.
The other man means well,
but you find his visits dull:
he doesn't talk, just drives.
Well, thank you; it's good to know
that whatever else I am,
at least I'm not a bore —
except that this other man,
the fellow you describe,
he sounds a lot like me,
right down to the fact that
he recently cancelled coming,
because he'd caught a cold.
Perhaps there have always been two —
the person I think I am
and the one you complain about.
We give him another ten minutes

and when he still doesn't appear,
we drive to the café as usual.
Our talk, as always, proceeds in parallel,
you ignoring what I say.
I'm used to it — I'm your son —
but the stranger who takes you out,
he must be some kind of saint.
It's very dull being the other man.

Home

Casually, you ask me
if I'll describe for you
what your old house was like.
I hope my surprise doesn't show.

It's frightening to think
that forty years of your life
could suddenly just disappear
down some cognitive sink-hole.

Luckily, I've got with me
something I can show —
snaps I took on my smartphone
the last time I was there.

I'm pleased that my "parting shots",
only an afterthought then,
have come in useful now,
as I swipe through the pictures with you.

Everything looks as it should:
the garden's neat and tidy,
though autumn has been through
and stripped the poplars bare.

My car parked on your drive
and the curtains we left up
(part of the deal, plus carpets)
help make the place look lived in.

No one would know
that only the day before
the house-clearer had been in
and emptied everything out —

a lifetime's worth of junk,
stuff we didn't want,
things you'd forgotten you had,
before the forgetting began.

Home Entertainment

You've forgotten how things work.
It was rote learning in your day,
not all this multiple choice
and menu screens confuse you.

Even when you lived at home,
you wanted it all spelt out.
Each time I came, I'd dictate
more instructions for you to mislay.

It was simpler when all we had
were the wireless and gramophone.
So many gadgets now and none of them
with names, only a scrabble of letters.

The grand plan you had
of methodically working through
the mature Mozart operas on disc
died with *Die Entführung*.

They were "an interest" you said,
the hobbies you had when Dad died,
picked up then suddenly dropped
quicker than childhood crazes.

There's not much that interests you now.
You can't read without losing the plot
and complain television's too tame,
even detective series.

A mystery, that, in itself,
until I realised, of course,
you're in bed by the watershed;
this was daytime TV.

Radio was more your thing.
Reception up North had been good,
beamed out from Winter Hill.
Down here, it was fuzzy, soft.

We bought you a state-of-the-art
digital-radio set, complete with auto-tuning
and push-button pre-select,
easy to use, but beyond you.

Too many stations to choose from —
and those just the ones we'd set.
In the end, we taped everything up,
leaving you with a binary on-off.

Still Life

A laminated sheet lists
activities for April.
"I don't bother with that," you say.
"They're trying to baby me."

Well, Tai Chi in the lounge
or a pub night in with Dave
may not be quite your thing,
but there's plenty else besides:

garden walks with Pam,
or classical music with Jean,
or memories, Jean again.
(She's a busy one, that Jean.)

But no, you're adamant:
you'd rather be in your room
with the radio for company
than join in silly games.

Yet I've seen a photograph
of you with your white hair
practically flaring the shot,
a paintbrush in one hand,

your normally dull eyes
sharpened to a point,
as you put the final touch
to a daffodil you've drawn.

The outline looks a bit shaky,
but that may be just the breeze
and smearing the yellow a little
just makes it more radiant.

I want to tell you, "Well done!"
for coaxing your Welsh, spring flower
out from under forgetful snow,
but how dare I patronise?

The 3-D Clock

The Digital Dementia Day-clock
that I've ordered for you online
comes discreetly packed
inside an unmarked box.

No one mentions the D word —
by which I don't mean "digital" or "day" —
or cracks unsympathetic jokes
about needing a cuckoo clock.

I wrap it up as the perfect Christmas gift,
so it's less anonymous.
It may not be just what you wanted,
but it's certainly something you need.

You give the blank screen
an equally blank look.
"It's a clock, Mum, not a TV.
Watch while I plug it in."

It'll give you something to look at,
hours of entertainment,
only without the hours,
or minutes come to that.

It tells you the day of the week
and right now that it's "Afternoon".
(You couldn't have worked out the time
on a twenty-four-hour clock

and suggested two instead —
one for AM and one for PM —
though neither of us, to be fair,
could quite follow the logic through.)

You'll be back in the moment, Mum:
no more going in for breakfast,
when the others have finished their tea,
no more visitors "out of the blue".

But next time, you're still in bed
on what ought to be
a bright, clear "Thursday (Morning)" —
no sign of the clock anywhere.

"Oh, that thing," you say,
dismissively waving your hand.
"I couldn't get used to it.
It's worse than one that ticks."

Night-time for you meant the dark,
not "Night" spelt out clear as day
on a lit screen that never let up.
You'd rather stay unenlightened.

Nonage

"People are always surprised,"
I remember you telling me once,
"when I say how old you are."
Well, not as surprised as I am,

but why would they think that, Mum?
Were you lying about your own age,
the way you deceived yourself
about how old you looked?

Or was it the habit you had
of referring to us as "the children",
even though my sister and I
have grown-up kids of our own.

It was always "the" children, too,
rather than "my" children.
Whose issue we were
apparently wasn't the issue

so much as minority.
You a nonagenarian now
and the two of us still in our nonage?
Who's going to fall for that?

You just didn't want to let go.
Only now that you've lost your grip
on things in general,
do I know what it's like to feel free.

When sometimes you look at me
like a stranger you recognise,
but somehow can't quite place
and think it's rude to say,

my feeling is one of relief.
What might be a bad day for you
is bound to be better for me —
you were always polite to strangers.

See Me After

Teaching was in your blood —
you had red ink in your veins.
Cigarette in one hand,
a pen poised in the other,

you'd attack the marking pile.
Tick, cross, underline,
"Good work," "Must improve,"
your default mode: exasperation.

In the end, when words really did fail you
and I had to help you out,
you still picked me up on mine.
"The man who does odd jobs?"

"A janitor," I suggest.
"Yes, yes, but the *English* word.
You watch too much TV."
Alright, a caretaker then.

It's just as well you can't see
that it isn't spelt "all right".
I used to resent your corrections.
These days I'm glad you still care.

You wouldn't be you,
if you weren't the one in charge.
After you went into care,
it was only a matter of time

before you assumed some role,
institutions being all alike.
Accompanist I could believe,
but "Lecturing, Mum? On what?"

In the end, when your dreamed-up tasks
became too much to bear,
you demanded to see the warden
to hand in your notice to quit.

Anomia

Even the words for ordinary,
everyday things are beginning to fail you now
like old labels that come unstuck
and get muddled beyond recall.
I do my best to help you,
as together we puzzle out
what exactly it is you mean.
It isn't an easy task —
I'm not a mind-reader, Mum,
and you don't give me much to go on.
Your periphrases, though accurate enough,
are somehow beside the point.
"The thing that holds water," you say,
I lamely render as "jug",
only to find it was "radiator" you meant.
There's even a name for it,
a word for the loss of words,
though it isn't one I use.
I work around it instead,
not wanting to worry you.
"It's just old age," I say,
"or because you're feeling tired."
You seem satisfied with that,
though you've seen it happen before —
to your sister and some of your friends.
We don't need words for it,
this thing that's bothering you;
we both know what it means.

Con Moto

Who else would have thought of it:
teaching yourself to drive
by sitting at the piano,
playing with (look!) no hands?

That's how I found you one day,
both feet on the pedals,
an umbrella clutched by your side,
as you practised changing gear.

In the days before simulators,
what else were you to do?
And I needn't have scoffed (so there!):
you passed your test first time,

even though years of driving
never quite smoothed out
those kangaroo starts
and tooth-on-edge, grinding gears.

You carried on into your eighties,
pooh-poohing my spoil-sport advice
about buses and taxis being cheaper
(and less costly to life and limb).

Nothing could dent your resolve.
Wing mirrors in the end
became consumable items,
the same as touch-up paint.

Even writing your car off once,
not stopping when you should,
didn't prompt you to give it up,
whatever that policeman said.

Those white-knuckle rides to the station!
I'd rather have walked through the rain
with a ton of luggage in tow
than have taken those lifts with you.

"Remind me again," you said,
as we came to a busy junction,
"what happens at roundabouts."
No arguing, you were grounded after that.

You still had the piano, though,
tuned up, ready to go,
whenever you fancied a spin,
or a trip down memory lane.

You read music better than roads
and never lost your touch,
the notes still at your fingertips,
long after you'd failed to grasp words.

Mother Tongue

Tonight, you're speaking Welsh,
just a few, short, tentative phrases,

words of greeting perhaps,
or bits of maternal advice.

Mum, I don't understand you.
Don't you understand?

"It's Welsh, her first language,"
I tell the foreign nurse.

Speaking it seems to calm you.
Welsh was the language of home,

a refuge from the English
of teachers and bullies.

Whoever you think I am,
Mum, I'm on your side.

I wish I could tell you
you're safe here in hospital.

I'd like to think that in Welsh
you're making sense.

Voicemail

You've taken to leaving
silent messages
on my voicemail at home.

When I realised it might be you,
I dialled to trace the call,
then rang you back myself.

"Did you try to phone me, Mum?"
"I don't know." There's a pause.
"Perhaps I might have done."

I recognise them now,
your recorded silences.
They've a quality all of their own,

a subtly different sound
from computers cold-calling me
or plain wrong numbers.

First, there's a puzzled silence,
then a silent pause
and the clunk as you hang up.

You used to leave me tit-bits
from "The Times" — tips on things
such as etiquette or health.

I stopped listening years ago.
Only now you've nothing to say
do I strain to hear everything.

On the Ward

On the geriatric ward,
everyone makes sense
of their own reality.

That man's name being called
over and over again
isn't going to bring anyone back.

The woman singing songs
thinks she's in a pub
on which time was called years ago.

Your neighbour I thought was sane
now tells me her father's coming
(she's eighty if she's a day).

And you, Mum. How are you?
Not in such a good place.
You seem agitated today.

"Swirling!" you say — and, "Dark!"
grasping the sides of the bed,
as if something's sucking you in.

Will waking you make it worse?
Are you actually asleep?
It's hard to tell these days.

I lean over to clasp your hand,
though I know you're out of reach
and way beyond rescue now.

Opening the Window the Night You Died

It was peaceful in the end.
You slipped away without fuss
so calmly at dead of night
that I might have missed the whole thing,

if the carer hadn't got up
and rushed across the room,
then wrenched hard on the latch,
so the window's jaw dropped open.

"I'm sorry; I'm superstitious,"
was all she said. Working somewhere like this,
she'd have seen death many times —
of course, she knew the lore.

She must have been afraid
that your shucked soul, trapped indoors,
was going to become the care home's crotchety house-ghost,
scaring old people already out of their wits.

Even after I knew you'd gone,
it was hard to believe you weren't there —
your hand still warm in mine,
despite the room's mortuary chill.

You were always opening windows —
fresh air was good for us —
so I hoped you wouldn't mind
that I didn't want it shut.

I thought of the dead doing it for their dead,
a chain of obligation stretching back down the years,
unbroken since the year dot —
or, at least, since there have been windows.

Your Funeral

You were funny about funerals,
had Dad shuffled off
with the minimum of fuss,
after his heart-attack,

then refused to attend your sister's
(Scotland being too far),
despite all those lectures we had
about keeping the family close.

You must have been haunted
by something more than death
to have tried to dodge your own
by leaving your body to science.

It's your funeral, we joked,
forgetting that we, the bereaved,
were the ones who'd be left in limbo,
until they released your remains.

When, in the end, the hospital
wouldn't take you (no good
for teaching — the brain itself
wouldn't make sense),

we did the best we could
to let you have the last word,
arranging a simple send-off:
no clergy, no eulogy, no wake,

just our own choice of music and readings
and only the family there
to witness that glitch at the close,
which I know you would have hated,

when "Nimrod" played on a loop
kept everyone in their seats,
only stopping when I stood up —
like a game of un-musical chairs.

The Author

Stephen Claughton was born in 1951 and grew up in Manchester. He read English at Oxford and worked for many years as a civil servant in London. Twice nominated for the Forward Best Single Poem Prize, his poetry has appeared in both print and online magazines, including *Agenda*, *Atrium*, *The High Window*, *Ink Sweat & Tears*, *The Interpreter's House*, *London Grip*, *Magma*, *Poetry Salzburg Review*, *The Poetry Shed* and *The Warwick Review*. His first pamphlet, *The War with Hannibal*, was published by Poetry Salzburg in 2019.